NIDHI CHANANI

**KASSANDRA HELLER**

Apartment in the Land of Ooo

STEPHANIE BUSCEMA

Summer Time

PHIL RYNDA

Summer Time

MAHENDRA SINGH

Ooozymandias

THE LITTLE FRIENDS OF PRINTMAKING

Treehouse

FINN THE HUMAN

TONY MILLIONAIRE

Finn the Human

**JJ HARRISON**

Simon and Marcy

MAHENDRA SINGH

Caravan

PHIL McANDREW

JJ HARRISON

STEVE CONLEY

JON VERMILYEA

TINY KITTEN TEETH

Fionna & Cake

SCOTT C.

CHRYSTIN GARLAND

ELEANOR DAVIS

KEVIN WADA

ANDREW GROVES

Billy the Hero

OLLY MOSS

Finn